Distributed in the United States by
Smart Apple Media,
1980 Lookout Drive,
North Mankato,
Minnesota 56003

Text copyright © Linda Bygrave
Illustrations copyright © Louise Voce

Consultant: Michael Chinery

ISBN 1-93198-353-4
Library of Congress Control Number 2003102391

Printed in China

I am a Rabbit

Written By
Linda Bygrave

Illustrated by
Louise Voce

Chrysalis Education

I am a rabbit.
I am small with two long ears,
thick fur, and strong back legs.

I also have a short, white fluffy tail.

I like to hop about.
The thick hair on the soles
of my feet gives me a good grip.

My thick coat of fur protects
my body. It grows even thicker
in winter to keep me nice and warm.

I like to live with lots of friends.
We eat and play in grassy places.

I make my home under the ground.
It is called a burrow.

This is my burrow with places to run
and places to pass each other.

There are also rooms for sleeping
and a nursery for the babies.

I stay in the burrow most of the day.
I come out at night to feed and play.

I use my teeth and claws to keep myself very clean.

Most of the time, I eat grass.
But I also eat the farmer's vegetables
if I can find some.

In winter, when there is no grass
or vegetables, I eat the bark
from trees.

I am a mommy rabbit.
Over there is a daddy rabbit.
We look quite alike, don't we?

We're feeling excited because
we are going to have some babies.
Lots and lots of babies!

I have my babies when it is warm.
Usually, I have between three and
eight of them at once.

Each lot of babies is called a litter.
At first, they can't see or hear.

After about ten days my babies can see.
Now they have more fur
and they can move and hear well.

Once they are about two weeks old,
we leave the burrow for the first time.
We meet lots of other rabbits.

We must be careful! We have
enemies. If we keep very still,
it is hard for them to see us.

I can move my ears backward or forward
without moving the rest of my body.
This way I can hear if an enemy is coming.

My eyes are on the sides of my head.
I can keep a lookout all around me
without moving my head.

If an enemy does come near, the oldest daddy rabbit thumps the ground hard with his feet. Then we all run home.

When they are one month old,
my babies can look after themselves.
They don't need me anymore.

I carry on feeding and playing,
and having more babies.
That is why there are so many rabbits.
Good-bye!

ML   2/04